PRAYER

MOVING WITH THE SPIRIT TO RENEW OUR MINDS, BODIES, AND CHURCHES

AND FASTING

DAVID ROADCUP & MICHAEL EAGLE

FOREWORD BY SHODANKEH JOHNSON

I want to dedicate this volume to the kingdom warriors and fellow soldiers whom the Lord has led me to disciple over the years. Courage and faithfulness to each of you, my brothers and my sons.

— David

I would like to dedicate this to my wonderful and godly wife Michelle, who has helped show me the true heart behind fasting; to my beautiful daughter, Courtney, whose intellect and joyful pursuit of Jesus has inspired me in many ways; and to Mason, of whom I am proud and for whom I am so grateful to God that he gifted me with a son like you.

— Michael

CONTENTS

FOREWORD

This book reintroduces us to two vital acts that connect us directly with our God. We can think of fasting as a brush that removes obstacles in our path to God and prayer as our line of direct communication with him, like a direct telephone line. If fasting clears the way to communion with God, prayer is the key to the door of his heart.

Written with simplicity and honesty, David Roadcup and Michael Eagle invite us into two Christian principles which are among the most important pillars of Christian practice. As humans, we are very imperfect. We are inundated with worldly distractions from every angle, yet we are graciously invited into close communion with our God. This communion is what we are made for and what we must practice. Through prayer and fasting, we can move on from dabbling in Christianity and can move onward in our faith. This book will help enable those who have been previously inhibited to take the next steps into Christian maturity and communion with God to do just that.

We are created to worship God and enjoy his goodness. Jesus said that his Father is always looking for "true worshipers" (John 4:23). In order for us to become what our Father seeks, fasting and prayer are foundational—for they bring us into the humble posture of worshipers who desire to know the heart of the Father.

The disciplines of fasting and prayer blend people's spiritual hunger with God's spiritual dynamism. This book by David and Michael show us how we can realistically pursue these two disciplines. *Prayer and Fasting* is every Christian's handbook for spiritual renewal.

Bravo to my Christian brothers for this. By your book, you have pointed us to the tried-and-true path to the blessed life on earth. Likewise, these principles help us rely on the Spirit's power in disciple-making movements, a power which is able to lead many people to a paradise existence in the heavens.

— Shodankeh Johnson, International
Disciple-Making Movement Leader and Trainer,
New Harvest Ministries

INTRODUCTION

Why write this book on prayer and fasting? The answer is simple: we are ready to see revival.

We are writing from an American context, where too many Christian leaders have made an uneasy peace with the way things are. As long as people keep coming to church and they seem happy enough, we find ourselves feeling fine about the status quo. This complacency is foreign to the urgency and passion of Jesus and His apostles that we read about in Scripture. When we compare the apostles' zeal for spreading the gospel with our contentedness in maintaining church memberships, we come to see our desperate need for revival. To be precise, we desperately need revival to start *in us*.

If we want to see revival, then we *must* begin seriously praying and fasting. But serious prayer and fasting are practices which require effort and self-discipline. It's difficult enough getting church people to attend a Sunday morning service! How are we going to encourage regular prayer and fasting in an era of distraction, busyness, and spiritual apathy?

This book remains realistic about the many challenges that can derail our prayer and fasting. However, the book is hopeful and winsome as it walks the reader through the practical steps of becoming individuals and churches that take seriously prayer and fasting. This short handbook describes the kinds of practices that position us to become faithful seekers of God—the kind of practices God has historically used as the spearhead for revival.

A revival or season of renewal has never taken place without being ushered in with seasons of prayer and fasting on the part of faithful servants of Jesus. Looking back at history through the great periods of revival, believers gathered into groups, sought the Lord, and asked for His refreshing presence. They asked for a movement that reached far beyond what could be accomplished by effective planning and good strategy (although there is nothing wrong or unspiritual about strategy and planning!). They asked for a movement of the Holy Spirit, for a visitation of God's presence, which would bring about genuine repentance, nurturing, and blessings from our Father.

They sought something beyond worship and ministry as usual.

Pastor Ronnie Floyd once wrote of the gathering spiritual darkness and the church's increasing paralysis in the face of it. He concluded, "The answer to our spiritual crisis will come when we put off our mindsets of self-worship, territorialism, and the spirit of arrogance and pride, and put on the sackcloth of prayer and fasting and humiliation and repentance before God."[1] Today we are in desperate need for this same visitation from our Father. How desperately we need His touch in our churches, cities, and states. When we have a major prayer movement in action—forging forward through the power of the Holy Spirit—and we combine that prayer with fasting, we can and should expect powerful, impactful things to happen. It has happened in the past and it can happen now! But we must pray and fast, to seek the Lord and His visitation.

In our milieu today, we need for the church to be revived and also matured. We need believers who are growing in their faith and ministry. This will come only when ministry leaders and lay leaders in our churches begin using the relational discipling approach taught to us by our Lord Jesus Christ. Our current ministries, as in the past, are producing many good results. We need to now move to the next level and begin relationally discipling believers, especially in the spiritual disciplines of prayer and fasting. Churches that regularly pray and fast will become a support system for the revival which we are asking the Lord to send.

To this end, we offer this short book. We begin by describing our central, daily connection with God: *prayer*. Then we move onto how we can accompany the sweet fellowship of prayer with the self-denial of fasting. May the following words be received as more than interesting insights. May they motivate practices which fuel revival.

THE PRACTICE OF PRAYER

"Now He was telling them a parable to show that at all times they ought to pray and not to lose heart."
– Luke 18:1, NASB

"The effective prayer of a righteous man can accomplish much."
– James 5:16, NASB

The grand experience of coming into the presence of the creator of the universe can be a truly amazing moment. Pause and think about what prayer is: we are invited into our Father's throne room to witness His glory, to marvel at His majesty, and to be deeply impacted by the truth and reality of who our Heavenly Father is! We are welcomed to share in one of the deepest experiences of our spiritual lives. What an honor! What a privilege!

Yet sometimes, what a challenge!

While regular prayer can be hard work, it is a rewarding and critical discipline for any leader to cultivate. It is the power source for our ministry and our lives. It is our breath, our food, and our main line of communication to the God who loves us. Prayer is our lifeline to God.

God reaches down to us through grace and we reach up to Him through our genuine faith. Our faith leads us to prayer. We receive His grace through our faith and express our love through our prayer.

The witness to prayer, examples of prayer, and instructions about prayer are emphasized throughout the pages of Scripture. We are encouraged, taught, and called to this vital discipline.

As we think about discipling men and women in Jesus, prayer should be the foundation for this effort. We depend on different strategies to make disciples and grow our churches. This is fine and a part of our ongoing work in Christ's name, but we must understand that prayer is the *main* strategy when it comes to building the kingdom. Our efforts are welcomed by God. He has chosen to work through us as His servants. But the heart of our work and effort must begin with prayer.

In his excellent book on prayer, *Extreme Prayer*, Greg Pruitt observes, "I decided to search Scripture to discover the kinds of prayers that God has promised to answer and then to focus our whole mission on praying those prayers. Prayer became our strategy. The power unleashed by this approach had made me want to pray longer and more often. I've come to see prayer as *the* work."[2] Could it be that if church leaders adopted prayer and seeking our

Heavenly Father's face as our main work, earth shaking happenings would begin taking place in our ministries?

In this section, we will examine several aspects of prayer and its place in the lives of those who lead and make disciples. These aspects will include specific *reasons* why we pray, the *examples* of Jesus who taught us to pray, *hindrances* to effective prayer, and *steps* to developing a prayerful life. As you will see, prayer is indeed the power source for those who wish to lead in the spirit of Christ. We will follow this section on prayer with a section describing the forgotten but powerful discipline of fasting.

REASONS TO PRAY

In what follows, we want to share with you two of the most fundamental reasons we pray.

God Calls Us to Pray

The first reason to pray is that God, our Heavenly Father, created the medium of prayer. It was His decision to make an open line of mental, emotional, and spiritual communication with mankind. From the beginning, the Father has desired to have a positive and healthy relationship with His people. In the Garden of Eden, God came in the cool of the day to see Adam and Eve (Genesis 3:8–9). It is amazing to think that the Creator of the universe was seeking out man and woman. He desired to connect with them and wanted to cultivate a relationship with them. He desires the same today with His children.

It is a significant point to remember that *no relationship on earth can be sustained without communication.* This is one of the reasons that prayer is so important to our Father. Communication is the lifeblood in all relationships; it is one spirit, heart, and mind connecting to another. Richard Foster rightly observes, "Of all the spiritual disciplines, prayer is the most central because it ushers us into perpetual communion with the Father."[3] Our Father created this concept and He is asking us to practice it, as well. Our Father loves our prayers! Proverbs 15:8 (NASB) says, "The sacrifice of the wicked is an abomination to the Lord, but the prayer of the upright is His delight."

It is no wonder that a loving Father desires this communication; consider some of the transformation that comes about through prayer: Through prayer, the lifting of our minds, hearts, and souls to God brings us into His presence. Through prayer, we grow in our love, devotion, and commitment to Him. Through prayer, we connect with Him. So today, God is calling us to pray. He is calling us to come to Him and receive a renewed spirit, to be in His presence and enjoy refreshing, encouraging, nurturing times with Him.

Jesus Gives Us an Example to Pray

We discover a second fundamental reason to pray when we look at the life of Jesus. A fitting question when studying the life of Jesus would be to ask what, from His life and ministry, Jesus thought was important. What did He model and emphasize? We know that living a life of holiness and purity was important to Him. We know that believing in God as our Father and Himself as the Son of God was important. Justice, mercy, faith, and truth were important factors in His thinking.

We also see from His example that Jesus placed a high premium on the practice of prayer. It was not an afterthought to Him but a main staple of His life and ministry. Prayer was of primary importance to Jesus.

The great prayer writer, E.M. Bounds, makes this observation:

> The praying of Jesus was real. No man prayed as He prayed. Prayer pressed upon Him as a solemn, all-imperative, all-commanding duty, as well as a royal privilege in which all sweetness was condensed, alluring, and absorbing. Prayer was the secret of His power, the law of His life, the inspiration of His toil and the source of His wealth, His joy, His communion, and His strength. To Christ, prayer occupied no secondary place, but was exacting and paramount, a necessity, a life, the satisfying of a restless yearning and a preparation for heavy responsibilities. Closeting with His Father in counsel and fellowship, with vigor and in deep joy, all this was His praying.[4]

Consider how much of Jesus' ministry was fueled by prayer. Tim Keller, in his excellent book on prayer, points out the frequency and impact of prayer in Jesus' life. He writes:

> Jesus Christ taught his disciples to pray, healed people with prayers, denounced the corruption of the temple worship (which, he said, should be a 'house of prayer'), and insisted that some demons could be cast out only through prayer. He prayed often and regularly with fervent cries and tears (Heb. 5:7), and sometimes all night. The Holy Spirit came upon him and anointed him as he was praying (Luke 3:21–22), and he was transfigured with the divine glory as he prayed (Luke 9:29). When he faced his greatest crisis, he did so with prayer. We hear him praying for his disciples and the church on the night before he died (John 17:1–26) and then petitioning God in agony in the Garden of Gethsemane. Finally, he died praying."[5]

As He demonstrated from the beginning of His ministry (Luke 3:21) all the way to the cross (Luke 23:46), Jesus our Lord clearly understood the importance of prayer in His experience here on earth. After His public ministry began, His schedule was intense and His time was dramatically pressured. In the midst of all of the need around Him, He still specifically planned times for meeting with His Heavenly Father (Matt. 14:23; Mark 1:35; Luke 5:16; 6:12; 6:46; 9:18). He worked at opening space for this important discipline. He would leave the crowds and even His apostles, going to a quiet and lonely place, to create time for communication with His Father. He would get up early, stay up late (sometimes all night) and not allow the pressure of His schedule or the demands of people to stop Him from this appointed time.

Jesus clearly models the great importance of maintaining and nurturing this connecting link. Because it was a major priority for Him, He worked at making time. What a dramatic lesson for us who live pressured lifestyles today! If Jesus modeled this with such emphasis, we must understand how important prayer should be in our lives as we follow His sacred example.

Even as we understand God's call to pray and seek to imitate Jesus' example in prayer, we need to be realistic that cultivating a life of prayer (and fasting too, as we will see) is challenging. It is important to recognize and anticipate these challenges if we want to overcome them and become faithfully Christlike in our prayer.

HINDRANCES TO PRAYER

As we grow in our experience of prayer, we discover that our prayer times can be times of struggle and even frustration. Hindrances present themselves to block our effectiveness as prayer warriors. Distractions of all kinds arise.

Roadblocks appear to slow down our prayer effectiveness or even attempt to stop it altogether. This is not surprising due to the fact that the evil one is constantly doing everything he can to stop the prayer life of the Christian.

E.M. Bounds states, "Prayer in the Old Testament is called 'wrestling.' Conflict and skill, strenuous, exhaustive effort are involved. In the New Testament we have the terms striving, laboring, fervently, fervent, effectual, agony, all indicating intense effort put forth, difficulties overcome."[6]

The first major hindrance to prayer is the spiritual warfare that comes from Satan.

Attack in Spiritual Warfare

It is important to realize upfront that a major hindrance (and something which will no doubt utilize and exacerbate other hindrances) is spiritual warfare. Satan desires to disrupt your connection with God. Thus, a critical part of utilizing prayer and fasting in our lives and ministries is understanding the reality of spiritual warfare in the battle for the souls of men and women. Satan is real and has a plan to thwart any and all attempts to bring glory to our Father and to build His Kingdom.

Satan knows that prayer is one of our major weapons against him. It is a powerhouse of protection against our foe: "The opposition of Satan to prayer comes because prayer is a powerful spiritual weapon given to Christians that unleashes the power of Jesus Christ and can bring defeat to our enemy."[7] Satan must feel especially threatened by fervent prayer on the part of leaders. He knows that strongholds are damaged or torn down when leaders pray. He knows that people are led to salvation when leaders pray. He knows that ministers are empowered to preach life-changing sermons when leaders pray. Satan is dismayed when he sees disciples meeting with and teaching other disciples to pray. He knows that Christians and their churches are nurtured and challenged when leaders pray. Satan trembles when groups of leaders gather together in prayer in a home, a church conference room, or in a retreat center. Satan will do everything he can do to keep us from praying. This is the reality of our first hindrance to prayer, attacks in spiritual warfare.

When a Christian bows the knee and sincerely seeks our Heavenly Father's face, power breaks out. Imagine what happens when entire congregations begin seriously praying! Because a praying church threatens Satan, that church can expect increased opposition. Wesleyan minister Samuel Chadwick once said, "The one concern of the devil is to keep Christians from praying. He fears nothing from prayerless studies, prayerless work and prayerless religion. He laughs at our toil, mocks our wisdom, but he trembles when we pray."[8]

We know who Satan is and what his goals are for every person. Jesus Himself told us in John 10:10 (NASB) that "the thief comes only to steal and kill and destroy." We know what our enemy wants to accomplish in each of our lives, our families, and our ministries. He will do everything he can to stop our times of prayer. One of my mentors in ministry, Dr. Garland Bare, stated, "If there were no other reason to prove the existence of Satan other than the extreme difficulty I have developing a good prayer life, that would be sufficient."[9] We must understand that all the powers of hell are against our prayer lives.

There are several ways in which Satan attacks in spiritual warfare, and these all connect in various ways to prayer:

- *He wants us to ignore our spiritual resources.* Satan's greatest desire is to have us ignore and not utilize our spiritual resources. He wants us to fight in the flesh and not use the weaponry, such as prayer, that our Father has provided for us.
- *He will want us to ignore our own personal spiritual development.* When Christians grow in their spiritual lives, we pose a stronger threat to him. He will stop at nothing to keep us in a prayerless spiritual rut, to dull our edge, and to slow down our journey toward spiritual maturity and strength.
- *He will use criticism against us.* Criticism is one of Satan's major tools. It impacts our forward momentum, drains us emotionally and challenges

our confidence in God's call for our lives. We must understand that when we are doing kingdom work, the question is not, *Will we be criticized?* The question is, *How often and with what intensity will we be criticized?* Criticism is just part of kingdom work. It can be one of Satan's most effective tools. We must understand that to produce fruit in the kingdom, we must develop a thick skin while maintaining a soft heart. It is one of the keys to successful disciple making and productive ministry. When we tie our identity to popular opinion, we can become discouraged and less likely to feel right about boldly entering God's presence as beloved children.

- *He will use suffering or tragedy against us.* Whether it is ill health, a house fire, the loss of a loved one, a firing, or some other form of suffering, Satan uses these experiences to attempt to separate us from trust and confidence in our Heavenly Father. We will all go through "Job experiences" in our journeys through life. Knowing how to go through the fire with our Heavenly Father by our side is a key to surviving suffering as spiritual warfare. When we suffer, we must not let it keep us from prayer.

- *Busyness.* Satan uses busyness and over-scheduling to move us away from our devotional times and the most important things of our work. His main tactic is found in the fact that the things in which we are involved are all good things: family, ministry, work, hobbies, interests, etc. They are all good. The problem comes when there is too much on our plate to manage effectively. We must continually ask ourselves the question, *What are the most important things in my life?* We must focus on the most important. The old adage is true: "If Satan can't make you bad, he will make you busy." Tragically, when we become overly busy, prayer is the first practice to get cut.

So our first challenge is to understand that we have an enemy, and to know that he will do everything he can to prevent us from praying. He does this in various ways, described below. Some of these are not directly and always influenced by Satan, but Satan can use any of these to attack us on a spiritual level—and keep us from a fervent life of prayer and fasting.

Disobedience and Sin

A second challenge and major hindrance to prayer comes in our own disobedience. An obvious way in which disobedience keeps us from prayer is when we directly disobey God's command to pray. Yet there is another, less obvious way that disobedience threatens to keep us from praying. It is that when we give in to sin, we can find ourselves avoiding God and praying less. Recall Adam and Eve's reaction to God's presence when they disobeyed Him and then heard Him coming: "Then the man and his wife heard the sound of the Lord God as he was walking in the garden in the cool of the day, and they hid from the Lord God among the trees of the garden" (Gen. 3:8). When we have done what is shameful, it is often more natural to run *from* God than *to* Him.

Guilt can present a serious problem in the flow of our prayer. If we have unforgiven sin in our lives, the spiritual and emotional wall that guilt produces can keep us from connecting with the Lord. A thorough "spiritual house cleaning" on a regular basis is a good practice for all believers. The very best solution is to go to the Lord with a genuine spirit and pour out the confession of our sin to Him. 1 John 1:5–10 promises He is always willing to forgive us our sins. If several days have passed since prayer and guilt is holding you back, crash through the wall in your spirit and mind! Tell God you are back and plunge in again.

Do not let guilt at any level keep you from connecting with the Father. If your guilt is coming from unconfessed, repeated, intentional sin, why not seek out a confidant and ask for help and encouragement? Accountability will help you grow through the sin area and find a breakthrough to open the flow of your prayer life.

Although shame tempts us to wall off from God, the reverse is also true: humble obedience encourages prayerful fellowship with God. A posture of obedience helps us to welcome prayer as a natural rhythm. In turn, prayer from a posture of obedience cannot help but fuel more obedience.

It may seem obvious, but anyone who claims to love Jesus should be characterized by obedience to Him. In her insightful book titled *The Freedom of Obedience*, Martha Thatcher defines obedience in this manner: "Obedience is the prompt, personal response of an available life to God and His Word, always characterized by a focus on God and commitment to action."[10] Her use of the words, "prompt, personal response" describes with such precision what the Lord wants from us. When we are faced with a "Y in the road" in obedience to the Lord, He wants our *immediate* response to be according to His will and direction.

Another critical word in this definition is "available." When we come to Christ in obedience, we are to make ourselves completely available to the Lord and His will in everything. Her comment "focus on God" hits right at the heart of the obedience issue. In obedience, the focus is always on the Lord's will and leading, not on our own. The words "commitment to action" are the capstone as we consider that obedience always requires a decision and an action. We decide that we are going to follow Jesus at every turn. We commit to positive action whenever we are facing a decision about whether we will follow Jesus or whether we will have our own way.

Quite possibly, the most impacting request for an obedient heart on the part of all believers comes in John Chapters 14 and 15. Repeatedly Jesus tells the disciples that our love for Him will be indicated and measured by our personal obedience to what He asks us to do in following Him. Gary Johnson, a ministry colleague, reminds us, "If something in the New Testament is repeated, it's important!" In six different verses in John 14–15, Jesus tells us that if we love Him, we will keep His commandments (John 14:15, 21, 23–24 and 15:10, 14). What Jesus is saying is that the acid test of our genuine love for Him and commitment to Him is if we will keep His commands and follow what He has asked us to do. A faithful believer in Jesus obeys Him without hesitation because of their love for Him.

We must understand that this is a growth process. In his excellent book, *The Four Loves*, C.S. Lewis maintains, "Every Christian would agree that a man's spiritual health is exactly proportional to his love for God."[11] As the months and years pass in our devotion to Jesus, we also need to be growing in our prompt, heartfelt obedience to what Jesus daily asks us to do. We need to mature to the place where we love Jesus more than we love sin. The more maturity in obedience to Jesus, the more we will welcome prayer as fellowship with Someone we deeply love.

Interruptions and Distractions

Interruptions and distractions tend to happen on a regular basis when we attempt prayer. Whether it is a phone call or text, the dog, a knock at our door, or some other interruption, these occur regularly—especially when we resolve to pray.

As a professor at one of our Bible colleges, I (David) had an office in our main building that was located in an isolated part of the building. No one just "casually dropped by" on our wing. If you were in our location, it was because you were intending to be there. On a particular day, I had set in my schedule to have a quality worship time in the mid-to-late afternoon. This seemed like a good time of the day due to the fact that most of my colleagues had left for the day and students were either studying or working. From 8:30 a.m. to 3:00 p.m. that day, not one person had stopped by, nor had I received one phone call. I worked all morning, had lunch, and at 3:00 p.m., I tried to begin my scheduled communion with the Father. Yet from 3:00 p.m. until 5:00 p.m., I received numerous phone calls and several visits from students. This was not happenstance. Satan will use even well-meaning interruptions to disturb our prayer time.

We shouldn't allow calls, alerts, or texts on our phone to interrupt our prayer. Would we interrupt a visit with a Prime Minister or President because of a phone call? No way! If people call or text, we can respond to them when our prayer time is completed.

When Jesus instructed us about prayer, He taught us to "go into your room, close your door and pray" (Matt. 6:6). Perhaps one of the reasons was to help us manage distractions as effectively as possible. Determination and focus are key when we pray.

Out-of-Control Schedules

It is characteristic to our present culture that we are plagued with a busyness mentality. Our ministries, jobs, families, appointments, recreation, and other commitments constantly pressure us to meet their daily demands. It is the way we live. For many of us, our day planner is overflowing. In the midst of the helter-skelter, pressure-cooker schedules many of us keep, we must understand that if we do not carefully decide on what our main personal priorities are going to be and lay out our time and schedules based on these priorities, other people's needs and plans will determine our priorities and schedules for us. Many times, our time with God can become a casualty of our busyness. We fall into the trap of saying, "When things settle down" or "When my schedule opens up, I will find time." Jean Fleming observes, "I find myself thinking, *When life settles down I'll* . . . . But I should have learned by now that life never settles down for long. Whatever I want to accomplish, I must do with life unsettled."[12] We must carefully think through what is really important and how those most important things can be intentionally placed in our daily schedules.

The importance of a *plan* is the key to success when we talk about schedules. In his excellent book *Desiring God*, John Piper states:

> Unless I'm badly mistaken, one of the main reasons so many of God's children don't have a significant prayer life is not so much that we don't want to, but that we don't plan to. If you want to take a four-week vacation, you don't just get up one summer morning and say, "Hey, let's go today!" You won't have anything ready. You won't know where to go. Nothing had been planned. But that is how many of us treat prayer. We get up day after day and realize that significant times of prayer should be a part of our life, but nothing's ever ready. We don't know where to go. Nothing has been planned. No time. No place. No procedure. And we all know that the opposite of planning is not a wonderful flow of deep, spontaneous experiences in prayer. The opposite of planning is the rut. The natural, unplanned flow of spiritual life sinks to the lowest ebb of vitality. There is a race to be run and a fight to be fought. If you want renewal in your life of prayer, you must plan to see it.[13]

We must control our schedules and not let them control us. When we plan, we succeed many more times than not. Prayer then should find a high place on our list of daily priorities. It truly comes down to priorities and planning. If you're someone who writes in a pocket calendar, then pencil the prayer time in. If you schedule events in an online calendar, then schedule prayer time. You might even have someone check up with you periodically to see how well you are meeting your prayer goal. Whatever you do, do what it takes to make prayer a high priority—not just in your mind, but in your daily schedule.

Wandering Thoughts

The issue of having our minds wander while we are praying is nothing new. You know the situation: we begin praying in earnest and suddenly we find ourselves thinking of what we are going to have for dinner that evening or what our local sports team is doing that night.

At TCMI where I (David) serve as Professor of Discipleship, I have the great opportunity to teach a seminary class and lead seminars on the topic of spiritual formation. In discussing prayer in these sessions, I ask the members of the audience to raise their hand if they have a problem with their mind wandering when they pray. Invariably, almost everyone in the room raises their hand! Vast numbers of Christians struggle with the problem of their minds wandering, plus the disappointment or personal negative feelings that occur when it happens.

We can agree on several conclusions about our minds wandering when we pray. First, that the Lord understands our struggle. He knows we have feet of clay. He knows that fatigue, worry, or some other issue takes our concentration to places we had not planned. We have come to believe that our Heavenly Father would rather have a sincere prayer from our hearts, broken up occasionally by an unplanned mental focus lapse, than have no prayer at all.

Second, maintaining the mental, emotional, and spiritual focus required by prayer requires a lot of effort. Prayer is work. It is understandable that we might take an unplanned mental break during the prayer time. We believe that the Lord is not nearly as concerned about our mental breaks as we are. After the break is over, why not come right back to where you left off and continue? You might want to think about verbalizing your prayers audibly—praying out loud. The idea of journaling or writing your prayers might also help with the problem of a wandering mind. Speaking of written prayers, it might also be helpful to periodically use an already written prayer, such as those we find in the Psalms, to help focus the mind.

Apathy

Apathy, or emotional hesitancy, is having undistracted opportunity to pray and just not feeling like you want to spend time in prayer. Possibly, watching TV or doing the lawn just seems more appealing to you at the moment. You haven't prayed yet, and still you just don't *feel* like praying.

If we are honest, we are willing to admit that this scenario happens to most of us. When it happens, the very best thing to do is go to the Lord and admit that you don't feel like having prayer at that time. Don't be hesitant to do this. The Lord already knows you are feeling the way you are. The best approach is to go to our Father and say, "Lord, I really don't feel like praying now. Give me the desire *to want to want* to pray." Ask the Lord to start your engine. To warm your emotions. To draw you near. During these times, listening to good praise music can also move your heart to seek the Lord in prayer. Sometimes the best thing we can do is do what we don't want to do and push through to His warm fellowship and acceptance.

C.S. Lewis experienced difficulty in prayer like we do. He went through the same struggles we have. Out of his experience, though, he offers hope in prayer as he describes how all the wishes and demands of life can come at us like "wild animals": "The first job of each morning consists simply in shoving them all back; in listening to that other voice, taking that other point of view, letting that other larger, stronger, quieter life come flowing in."[14]

Now that we have discussed hindrances to anticipate and overcome, it is time to move on to describing what a prayerful life can look like.

DEVELOPING A PRAYERFUL LIFE

If we're talking about the power of prayer, consider power from another area of life to put things in perspective: jet airplanes. The largest jet engine on American planes today is the General Electric GE90 series found on the Boeing 777-300 model aircraft. At 115,000 pounds of thrust and fan diameter close to 11 feet, these giants power large aircraft to fulfill their mission. They have the power to generate lift to enable the plane, its crew, cargo, up to 396 passengers, and all their baggage to travel thousands of miles, successfully arriving at its destination. Extreme power!

The jets mentioned above are innovative marvels, but, of course, they obviously pale in light of the awesome, all-encompassing power of our Heavenly Father! His power is unlimited, unmatched, and totally available to us as His children. We have the power to accomplish His ministry here on earth!

The Word of God is replete with observations and explanations of the power of God. From the beginning of Genesis through the unfolding of the history of Israel, we see God's power exhibited in the Old Testament. In the New Testament record, we again see God's overwhelming power displayed through the life and ministry of His Son.

The same power of God is available to us today! Paul emphatically states in Ephesians 3:20 (NASB), "Now to Him who is able to do far more abundantly beyond all that we ask or think, according to the power that works within us." This is an exciting verse for every leader and believer to internalize. He tells us that God is willing to do beyond what any one of us can ask, think, or even imagine! The Greek word Paul uses here for "abundantly" is the adverb *hyper-ek-perissou*. It is one of Paul's super-superlatives. It has been translated "immeasurably more" (NIV), "far more abundantly beyond" (NASB), or "infinitely more" (NLT). F.F. Bruce made this observation, "Has Paul sought too much from God for his fellow-believers—praying that they may be filled up to the level of the divine fullness? They might think so as they heard this letter read aloud, but Paul reassures them: it is impossible to ask God for too much. His capacity for giving far exceeds His people's capacity for asking—or even imagining."[15]

If we truly believe in the power of God, we will do what it takes to develop a life of prayerfulness.

Accessing God Through Prayer

The overarching, everlasting power of our Almighty God is with us and available to us. The critical question would be this: How can we access this power of God to live our lives, build His kingdom, and tear down the strongholds of the domain of darkness? There are certain responses on the part of God's children that move God to exercise His power. God responds to our seeking and requests when the Word of God is present in our lives (as Joshua 1:8 and Psalm 1:2 describe), but it must also be combined with fervent and passionate prayer.

Powerful, heartfelt prayer is a lifeline to the anointing of God. The early church in the book of Acts modeled this for us to understand today. At least twenty references in the Book of Acts tell us that prayer permeated the ministry and life of the early church. We are told that the early church "joined together constantly in prayer" (1:14), and that they "devoted themselves" to prayer (2:42). In response to their prayers, amazing things happened (Acts 4:31; 8:15; 10:30; 12:5).

Individual men and women must find it in their hearts and personal disciplines to powerfully pray daily. Leaders should call them to consider this. In his classic work on prayer, E.M. Bounds states:

> "What the church needs today is not more machinery or better, not new organizations or more and novel methods, but men whom the Holy Spirit can use—men of prayer, men mighty in prayer. The Holy Spirit does not flow through methods, but through men. He does not come on machinery, but

on men. He does not anoint plans, but men—men of prayer.[16]

Rather than making plans and praying afterward that God would use them, we need to become prayerful people who are constantly available for God's use.

When we pray daily and fervently, God moves in our lives, families, and ministries. When we are prayerless, we grind out our lives on our own. A prominent church leader has written, "Prayerless people cut themselves off from God's prevailing power, and the frequent result is the familiar feeling of being overwhelmed, overrun, beaten down, pushed around, defeated."[17] Many Christians fail to see the connection between their prayerlessness and feeling perpetually overwhelmed.

If we are to tap into the power of God to create genuine, Spirit-led revival in our time, we must personally pray. We desire God to bring a spiritual awakening that will dramatically impact communities, but it will not happen without us finding a way to lead our churches to serious, fervent, heartfelt prayer. The absence of powerful prayer is one of the reasons we do not see the power of God unleashed upon the church or our culture.

Praying in Community

We must pray as individuals, but churches must also pray corporately. Prayer must be a foundation when it comes to seeing the church impact the culture in which it finds itself. Yet extended times of corporate prayer are not usually found in most worship services. In my work, I (David) visit numerous churches a year and am in multiple worship services. Most churches will average between two and three minutes out of the typical, corporate worship service for prayer. (I would suggest you note the amount of prayer in your church's morning worship services.) Because prayer is one of the missing elements, we must adjust our present congregational paradigm and move our churches to a new level of prayer involvement and obedience. Our worship services need to be saturated with prayer.

So how do we include more powerful times of prayer into our typical worship services? I would suggest that you introduce increased times of prayer slowly over several weeks. In addition to ministers, there can be elders, ministry team leaders (deacons), and other lay people who lead in inspirational prayer experiences. Can extended prayer times truly be conducted in a church where longer times of prayer have not been the norm? I do believe that it can be done.

I was invited to bring several messages at a men's retreat in Latin America. Over 200 men were in attendance. In the first session on a Friday evening, the leader, one of the area ministers leading the service, announced that it was time for the evening prayer experience. I was anticipating a rather brief "evening prayer." Our leader, through the method of Suggestion Prayer, led the men in a twenty-five-minute prayer exercise! It was a very passionate and meaningful experience. I realized that we in North America have a lot to learn about how to make room for prayer as a top priority.

Since longer, more passionate times of prayer are not usually found in our morning worship services, we may need to do some re-planning. Our worship times may have to be modified. The time designated to our worship elements may have to be adjusted. Or we may have to lead our churches into expecting longer worship experiences than in the past. (Some readers might wonder at this point if the authors have lost their minds!) Please remember: *To see things happen in our church we have never seen before, we are going to have to do things we have never done before.* In our main worship services, prayer needs to become a stronger aspect of our coming before the Lord.

In our corporate worship services, in our church staff and elder's meetings, and in our small groups and other ministries, prayer must be a priority! We must meet and we must pray together. Abiding, powerful, and passionate prayer is the key.

It comes down to this observation: When there is a lack of prayer, there will be an absence of power. When there is an abundance of fervent, heartfelt prayer, God's power will be evident among us. And it will be awesome to see!

Implementing a Life of Fervent Prayer

So how do we develop a life of prayer like this? Sometimes the key to infusing our lives and churches with prayer is to just begin praying. We fight through the warfare and just pray. And we continue praying. Either in our personal prayer closet or as a team, we pray. But the key is in just praying. Just begin. Just pray. Just start. As one advertiser states, "Just Do It!"

Emilie Griffin observes this struggle when she writes,

> There is a moment between intending to pray and actually praying that is as dark and silent as any moment in our lives. It is the split second between thinking about prayer and really praying. For some of us, the split second may last for decades. It seems, then, that the greatest obstacle to prayer is the simple matter of beginning, the simple exertion of the will, the starting, the acting, the doing.[18]

Should we wait until we feel like praying in order to pray? No, says Richard Foster. "Prayer is like any other work," he explains. "Our prayer muscles need to be limbered up a bit and once the flood-flow of intercession begins, we will find that we feel like praying."[19] Just taking the first step in prayer and beginning, just starting, is many times the key to a wonderful prayer experience.

God has provided us with our armor and weapons, prayer being one of the foremost. We need to utilize the weapons He has prepared for us. Daily we must enter the battle focused and prepared to defeat the enemy through the power of Jesus our Lord. Prayer is one of the mightiest forces on earth. As we pray, we know that God moves. Let us use this force in our warfare as one of the tools for victory.

Combining Prayer with Fasting

As described in detail below, fasting is a great, practical way to come to the Lord in prayer. We tap into a significant spiritual resource when we dedicate a fast to our Father. Fasting is one of the most difficult and challenging of the spiritual disciplines, due to our physical, mental and emotional connection to food. If you have not yet begun weaving the impacting discipline of fasting into your spiritual life, let us strongly encourage you to begin incorporating fasting into your spiritual journey.[20]

In the midst of attacks from the evil one, Scripture teaches us how to protect ourselves, our families, and our ministries. The apostle John tells us to understand that we have the victory. In 1 John 4:4, he writes, "Greater is He who is in you than he who is in the world" (NASB). We must also know that the battle we fight is fought in the spirit, not in the flesh. Paul reminds us in 2 Corinthians 10:3–4, "For though we walk in the flesh, we do not war according to the flesh, for the weapons of our warfare are not of the flesh, but divinely powerful for the destruction of fortresses" (NASB). Among these weapons are prayer, the Word of God, and fasting. James tells us in James 4:7, "Resist the devil and he will flee from you" (NASB). Paul writes one of the most extensive sections in the New Testament in Ephesians 6:10–20 when he exhorts to understand the person of Satan and his activity (verses 10–12) and how to protect ourselves. He describes the armor of God and how we wear it (verses 13–17), and how we are to use the power of prayer to fight against his activity (verses 18–20).

Are you truly ready to engage the battle you enlisted in the moment you became a follower of Jesus? Then it is time to get serious about prayer and fasting. In this next section, we will describe fasting and its importance as we "fight the good fight" (2 Tim. 4:7).

DISCUSSION QUESTIONS

1. What drew you to want to read a book on prayer and fasting?
2. The quote on page twelve, from Greg Pruitt's book, *Extreme Prayer*, makes the point that prayer is not just part of our work, but that prayer *is* the work. What does he mean by this comment? How could this concept be applied to your church and work?
3. Jesus repeatedly escaped the crowd, and sometimes the disciples, to meet His Heavenly Father for a time

of prayer. If Jesus was fully God and fully man, why did He need to pray?

4. What is the greatest struggle you face, personally, in developing the kind of prayer life you would really like to have?

5. How does Satan attempt to use personal suffering or tragedy to blunt your prayer life?

6. What is the most effective way to control the problem of "wandering thoughts" while praying?

7. Why does a sincere believer experience apathy at times when it comes to prayer? What can help us the most when it comes to overcoming apathy towards prayer?

8. Why is developing a plan for prayer in the life of a believer such an important step in building one's prayer life?

9. If church leaders decided to dedicate more time to prayer in their public worship services, how could they accomplish this?

10. Exactly how does prayer bring the anointing of our Heavenly Father to our lives and ministries?

11. What do we do when it appears that God is saying *no* to a specific prayer we are offering?

12. What two things could you do this week to dramatically improve your personal prayer life?

SECTION 2

THE PRACTICE OF FASTING

"I have not departed from the command of His lips;
I have treasured the words of His mouth more than my
necessary food."
— Job 23:12, NASB

"God is more concerned with our character than our
comfort. His goal is not to pamper us physically but to
perfect us spiritually." — Paul Powell

"Man shall not live on bread alone, but on every word that
proceeds from the mouth of God."
— Matthew 4:4, NASB

To introduce the forgotten discipline of fasting, it might be helpful to employ a metaphor. This metaphor will come from the world of long-distance running. I (Mike) ran recreational marathons in my younger years, and I was always looking for an edge to help my performance in order to set a "PR" (personal record). Most runners know about hitting the dreaded "wall" around mile 20. Since a marathon is 26.2 miles, the question becomes how to gain the stamina to sustain a pace to polish off those dreaded final 6.2 miles to make it to the finish line in record time. By mile 20, the body is depleted of its carbohydrate fuel source from both stored liver and muscle glycogen. The only thing left to burn is fat, which unfortunately does not supply the needed punch like carbs do. So there is this thing called "carbo-loading" where an athlete can eat lots of pasta and carbs for a couple days prior to the race in order to top off the gas tank, so to speak.

I soon discovered a way to "super carbo-load." The method consists of purposefully and intentionally depleting all my liver and muscle glycogen (carb) stores by switching to a diet of protein in the final week before the grand event. Then, two days prior, I would run, swim, and exercise intensely to use as many muscle groups as possible to force myself into carb starvation mode. By doing this, my body would produce certain enzymes so that when I finally did do my "super carbo-load," it would not only top off the tank, but essentially over-fill my tank to top capacity. This was done just before race day. That way, when race day came, I was supercharged to have maximum effectiveness and finish the race strong! Although the process was not easy, and the preparation was painful, it actually worked, and the benefits outweighed the temporary discomforts.

Fasting is much like this intentional depletion phase. It is not necessarily fun or pleasant, but fasting can open oneself to be super-filled with the presence of the Holy Spirit. This is like adding a megaphone to your time of prayer. Not only that, but fasting, as we will see, is a gift from God given to us to be filled with His Spirit instead of filled with ourselves. My hope is that you will get that "PR" (we will change the name to personal relationship) in your prayer time with God through fasting, and that in turn will bring Him much pleasure and glory. However, before we delve into what fasting is and its importance, it will be helpful to admit an obsession many of us have which will get in the way of fasting.

OUR IDOLATRY TO FOOD

Who doesn't like donuts? My (Mike) favorite flavor is a coconut-toasted, fully-loaded, right-out-of-the-oven, rich, delicious donut from my favorite shop. I also happen to love nachos, pizza, sushi, and the list definitely goes on. I received a rude surprise recently when I realized I was fifty pounds overweight and my BMI (body mass index) was in the obese range. *How did that happen?* Well, one of the biggest reasons (and one I had to repent of) was my obsession with food, especially as I looked toward food as a major answer to life's stress. In a real sense, food had become an idol for me. I desired to be healthy in mind, body, and spirit, but I had idolatry to deal with. *How could I break this cycle of idolatry?* As I learned, one of the Bible's answers to this kind of idolatry is the subject of this section of the book.

God intended food for our nourishment and even our pleasure (I am pretty certain those toasted coconut donuts will be in heaven). God created all good things and we, being created in His image, are custodians of what He has made. God granted us dominion over the earth and its creatures. Yet food can certainly become an idol. Although there was a lot more in play than a food craving, it is interesting that the first sin recorded in the Bible was connected to our appetite. We are made to crave our Creator. Anything other than God that we crave has the potential of becoming an idol, if we are not careful.

The concept of food taking top priority in life can also be seen in the story of Jacob and Esau. Esau, after coming home from the countryside, was tired and famished. Esau noticed that his younger brother, Jacob, had made some stew. Jacob offered to give Esau some of the stew—but only in exchange for Esau's birthright. As the Bible puts it, "Thus Esau despised his birthright" (Genesis 25:34b, NASB). Esau sacrificed what was most important for temporary satisfaction. He later regretted his decision. Throughout the Bible, God repeatedly teaches us to seek eternal rewards over seeking immediate satisfaction. The person who gives up something of temporal importance to grasp something of the eternal is a wise and discerning person. God calls us to sacrifice when drawing close to Him to experience His presence more powerfully. Through the practice of fasting, we are able to learn to sacrifice the temporary to see the larger picture of God's blessings.

The person who gives up something of great importance to grasp something of the eternal is a wise and discerning person. God calls us to sacrifice when drawing close to Him to experience His presence more powerfully.

We might be tempted to think of fasting as something antiquated. Make no mistake about it; fasting is ancient. Fasting has been a part of the history of religions and nations from the beginning of recorded time. Through the historical documents of ancient civilizations, we see that fasting was part of many ancient cultures. The Egyptians, the Greeks, and the Romans all observed fasting rituals. Early and later Jewish tradition called for fasting. Examples in the New Testament tell us that the Pharisees, the disciples of John the Baptist, and Jesus our Lord practiced this discipline. The New Testament church fasted. In the Middle Ages and into the eighteenth and nineteenth centuries, the great leaders of the church participated in fasting. Martin Luther, John Knox, Jonathan Edwards, and Charles Finney all encouraged their congregations and movements to utilize fasting. Is our time in history *less* idolatrous than these past eras? One could argue that our generation is especially prone to idolatry when it comes to prioritizing temporal pleasure over eternal joy. As such, we need to return to fasting more than ever.

As believers, our self-sufficiency, abundance, and fast-paced living have blinded us to deep spiritual realities. One of those realities is the forgotten or neglected act of obedience that comes through biblical fasting.

Christ-followers would do well to examine the discipline of fasting, keeping in mind its potential to bless us, our families, our churches, and our personal relationships with the Lord. It is truly one of the great practices, one that will engage us in our quest to love our Father better and reject idolatry.

FASTING — DEFINED AND EXPLAINED

A helpful way to approach fasting is to understand its definition. Significant leaders have defined fasting in the following ways.

Richard Foster defines fasting as "the voluntary denial of an otherwise normal function for the sake of intense spiritual activity."[21] Ronnie Floyd states that fasting is "the abstinence from food with a spiritual goal in mind or for a spiritual purpose."[22] Donald Whitney gives his definition and expands the thought when he writes, "A biblical definition of fasting is a Christian's voluntary abstinence from food for spiritual purposes. It is *Christian*, for fasting by a non-Christian obtains no eternal value because the Discipline's motives and purposes are to be God-centered. It is *voluntary* in that fasting is not to be coerced. Fasting is more than just the ultimate crash diet for the body; it is abstinence from food for *spiritual* purposes."[23]

It can also be helpful to look at the biblical words which are translated as "fasting." The Hebrew word used for fasting in the Old Testament is "tsom" (צוֹם). This word, used fourteen times, suggests "a period of complete abstinence from food and sometimes from drink undertaken as religious as plea to God."[24] The Greek word "nesteia" (νηστεία) is the New Testament word for fasting. Its primary meaning was "abstinence from food or drink or both for *health*, ritualistic, religious, or *ethical* purposes. The abstention may be complete or partial, lengthy, of short duration, or intermittent."[25]

Historically, fasting involves depriving oneself of food and drink. However, there are also additional ways to fast from things. Sacrificing things that are important and meaningful to us can provide a worthy substitution for food. Fasting from people or crowds or both is called *solitude*. Eliminating noise, hectic activity, and the din of the world is practicing *silence*. Technological devices such as our cell phones, computers, and tablets could be set aside for a specific time. We can fast from various forms of entertainment such as television, video gaming, and movies. We could fast from hurry, complaining, and expressing negative attitudes. Fasting from bitterness and unforgiveness could lead to significant emotional and spiritual healing. First Corinthians 7:4–6 tells us that married couples can agree to refrain from marital relations for a time for spiritual purposes. Paul teaches that this form of fasting should be mutually agreed upon with a start and finish time so as not to give Satan a place of power in spiritual warfare. In his excellent work on the Sermon on the Mount, Martin Lloyd-Jones states,

> To make the matter complete, we would add that fasting, if we conceive of it truly, must not only be confined to the questions of food and drink; fasting should really be made to include abstinence from anything which is legitimate in and of itself for the sake of some special spiritual purpose.[26]

As we develop an overview of the biblical concept of fasting, here is what we should understand. At its root, fasting is taking something highly significant to us and deciding to lay it aside or postpone it temporarily for a spiritual purpose. As you seek to learn more about fasting, consider the following characteristics of Christian fasting.

Fasting and our call to it is initiated by the leading of the Holy Spirit.
Fasting calls for a definite, proactive decision of obedience.
Fasting takes determination.

Fasting takes planning.

Fasting calls for using a "blow torch" to cut a place for a date in our planning calendars.

Fasting, if married, means communicating our plans to our family.

Fasting is not easy; it's hard, uncomfortable, sacrificial, and involves self-denial.

Fasting provides the opportunity to step out of our normal routines to gain a clearer perspective.

Fasting is a way to reboot the internal heart hard drive.

Fasting is one of the gateways to significant spiritual growth.

Fasting will stretch us to wonderful, new places of understanding and discernment.

Fasting is a form of worship and adoration.

Fasting involves prayer before our Father.

Fasting brings us into a world of wonder around our Father's throne.

Fasting is spiritually, mentally, and physically restorative.

Fasting exposes Satan's intense opposition to our desire to grow spiritually.

Fasting is normally surrounded by spiritual warfare. Plan on it.

Fasting brings power to prayer and to our ministries.

Fasting is an impactful experience, bringing blessing to us as God's children.
Fasting sincerely before our Father brings Him pleasure.

Our hope is to convince you that this ancient practice needs to be part of every believer's journey. We really can learn how to build this discipline into the ebb and flow of our normal schedules. By examining Scripture and the practices of saints who have gone before us, we can incorporate this ancient practice as part of our lives so that it can empower us for ministry and personal spiritual growth.

JESUS' EXAMPLE AND TEACHING ABOUT FASTING

Jesus' teachings about fasting in the Gospels are fairly brief. He did not give extensive information or exhortation on this topic. Most scholars believe this is due to the fact that the discipline of fasting was practiced widely over the Old and New Testament periods. Therefore, most people in that part of the world and historical period needed little instruction on the practice of fasting. Yet, even though His teachings in the Gospels are brief, we do know that Jesus both practiced fasting and taught us important facts about how to do it.

One of the things we love about Jesus is that He never asks us to do anything that He Himself is not willing to do. For example, Jesus taught His disciples to serve each other (Luke 22:26), something which He modeled the night before His crucifixion when He knelt down and washed His disciples' feet. In the same way, He called us to deny ourselves, take up our crosses, and follow Him (Luke 9:23). Modeling for us, again, He showed us how by going to the cross, denying Himself, and dying to save the world from sin.

Jesus teaches us fasting by example. He participated in a forty-day fast in the Judean wilderness in spiritual preparation for His public ministry. A forty-day fast would have been difficult, but not impossible, by taking water frequently. Matthew 4:1–11 gives us the account of Jesus successfully completing His fast and then successfully resisting Satan's temptations. In executing this fast, He was teaching us by His example that fasting needs to be part of the life of a believer who is seeking the Father.

Jesus not only modeled fasting, but He taught us about it as well. He teaches clearly about fasting in the Sermon on the Mount:

In Matthew 6:16–18, Jesus says,

> When you fast, do not look somber as the hypocrites do, for they disfigure their faces to show others they are fasting. Truly I tell you, they have received their reward in full. But when you fast, put oil on your head and wash your face, so that it will not be obvious to others that you are fasting, but only to

your Father, who is unseen; and your Father, who sees what is done in secret, will reward you.

Let's zoom in and look at the individual sections of Jesus' teaching here.

"When you fast . . . " (Matt. 6:16a).

Jesus begins this section, not by commanding His followers to fast, but by simply *assuming* that they *would* fast. Planned fasting days were very much a part of the religious culture and pattern of the temple leaders of Israel in Jesus' day. Luke 18:12 tells us that the Pharisees fasted two complete days a week. In addition, the disciples of John the Baptist also fasted on a regular basis (Mark 2:18). People knew what fasting was and how to do it. Rather than directly commanding His followers to fast, Jesus simply assumed that they would weave this practice into their discipline.

"Do not look somber as the hypocrites do, for they disfigure their faces to show others they are fasting" (Matt. 6:16b).

Many of the Pharisees during Jesus' time feigned religion but did not truly know God. Jesus pointed this out on many occasions (Luke 11:37–54; 20:9–19). They were expected to lead the people of Israel to God, but their hearts were terribly far from God and what He wanted. Going to the marketplace, they would use their fasting to get as much attention as possible. D.A. Carson observes that, "Such voluntary fasts provided marvelous opportunities for religious showmanship to gain a reputation for piety."[27]

Jesus speaks of them "neglecting their appearance." This would have involved not washing or combing their hair or using oils as a man's practice would have been at that time. They could have even gone so far as to sprinkle ashes on their heads. Jesus calls them "hypocrites" and condemns their show for attention.

The central issue is that the Pharisee's motives were vastly impure. They intensely craved attention and adulation from the people. They fasted out of hearts of darkness. Selfishness, self-centeredness, ego, and their insatiable drive for recognition drove their personal piety. They were rotten on the inside, where it truly counted. They had little interest in drawing close to their Heavenly Father through a heartfelt time of self-denial. They were interested only in the attention they could generate from the crowd. They wanted the veneration that people in the marketplace could provide. They were "full of the bones of the dead" (Matt. 23:27).

"Truly I tell you, they have received their reward in full" (Matt. 6:16c).

Jesus' comment here is a commentary on their motives. The Pharisees received what they wanted, the praise and adoration of men. It is a pity that the Pharisees, being so close to Life itself, missed the opportunity to know Him due to their rotten core of selfish desire.

We learn from this lesson, that when we come to the Lord with a fast, our hearts must be pure. Our main motive is to meet with the Lord in the fast where we draw close to Him. We seek His face, we love Him, we worship and adore Him. We are also to bring our requests to Him. It is our heart seeking His heart. Ronnie Floyd writes, "Fasting and prayer seasons are meant for reflection, celebration, and gratitude, carried out in a spirit of quietness—an unseen, unnoticed activity kept from the prying eyes of others, an experience to be enjoyed alone with God."[28]

> *"But when you fast, put oil on your head and wash your face, so that it will not be obvious to others that you are fasting, but only to your Father, who is unseen; and your Father, who sees what is done in secret, will reward you" (Matt. 6:17–18).*

Jesus concludes His teaching on fasting by giving direction to His followers on how to correctly fast. He asks us to anoint our heads and wash our faces so that we will not draw attention to ourselves in our fast. Our intent should be to minister before our Heavenly Father, seeking Him with the purest of motives. He desires sincerity and transparency from the deepest part of who we are.

Jesus tells us that if we fast secretly from our hearts, we can expect favor and blessing from our Father. Remember, *God always blesses obedience!*

To summarize, this teaching of Jesus on fasting in Matthew 6 tells us that He does want us to fast. In addition, He wants our motives to be pure as we seek our Heavenly Father through the means of fasting.

Jesus' second reference to fasting takes place in Matthew 9:15. He was answering a question from the disciples of John the Baptist about why Jesus' disciples were not fasting. Both the disciples of John and the Pharisees practiced fasting, but Jesus' disciples were not fasting. Jesus replies to their inquiry, "How can the guests of the bridegroom mourn while he is with them? The time will come when the bridegroom will be taken from them; then they will fast." Here Jesus uses the illustration of the wedding to communicate that during His public ministry time, the disciples (His "groomsmen") would not fast as the groomsmen at a Jewish wedding would not be fasting. Jesus continues by telling John the Baptist's disciples that after His resurrection, His disciples would be fasting.

Richard Foster points out the impact of this critical message in Jesus' teaching. He writes, "There is no way to escape the force of Jesus' words in this passage. He made it clear that He expected His disciples to fast after He was gone. Although the words are not couched in the form of a command, that is only a semantic technicality. It is clear from this passage that Christ both upheld the Discipline of fasting and anticipated that his followers would do it."[29]

In His two main teachings on the topic of fasting, Jesus shares critical direction. His instruction in Matthew 6 is extremely important due to the fact that Jesus is telling what kind of fasting our Heavenly Father wants from us. We want to follow His guidelines as carefully as possible. We also understand from Matthew 9 that while there is no direct command from Jesus to His followers to fast, He definitely expects them to lift the holy fast to our Father as an act of worship, devotion, and a request for His power to be manifested in our lives and work.

DIFFERENT TYPES OF FASTS

There are several different types or forms of fasting in which a believer might participate. Each has its own place, purpose, and expression of sincerity. Let's examine each of these forms from the Scriptural account.

The Normal Fast

The first type of fast is referenced as the *normal* fast. The normal fast involves setting aside food but not water. Any food or drink with caloric value is to be withheld. In pointing out that Jesus' fast in Luke was a normal fast, Arthur Wallis writes, "We are told that 'he ate nothing' (Luke 4:2), but not that He drank nothing. Afterwards it says 'he was hungry,' but not that He was thirsty. This all suggests that the fast was an abstaining from food, but not from water."[30] Since the human body cannot go more than several days without water, it is assumed that Jesus drank water during this time. There is also nothing to indicate that this was one of the miraculous fasts recorded elsewhere in Scripture. Jesus' fast would have been a normal fast.

The Partial Fast

The *partial* fast involves the giving up of certain foods or types of drink for a specific period of time. Certain foods are restricted, but all food is not stopped. It is simply the temporary setting aside of specified food items and specific drinks. We decide on one or more types of food and drink and do not partake of any of those items until the fast is completed.

Daniel clearly participated in the partial fast as recorded in Daniel 10:3. It would appear that Daniel usually conducted a normal fast, but in this case, changes his approach and does a partial fast. Daniel 10:3 tells us, "I ate no choice food; no meat or wine touched my lips; and I used no lotions at all until the three weeks were over." Giving up certain foods or drink for a period of time may seem a light form of fasting, but this is not always the case.

The Promise Keepers Men's Ministry had great impact in the 1990s. This ministry had men from every state in the nation and many men from other countries participating in their men's conferences in NFL stadiums across America. In 1997, P.K. invited a million men to join them in Washington, D.C. for a meeting called "Stand in the Gap." This was a clarion call to men to participate in a sacred assembly involving repentance and seeking the Lord for their families, churches, and their nation. P.K. was thrilled to see 1.6 million men on the mall in D.C. that day. Leading up to the event, the men guiding P.K. were challenged to conduct a fast (up to forty days) to the Lord for the event that would take place. I (David) called a good friend, one of the Vice Presidents of P.K., to ask him if he was going to participate in this fast. He told me that he was planning to participate in a partial fast for forty days. I requested permission to ask what he was planning to sacrifice for that fast. He had decided to give up meat, bread, coffee, and desserts for forty days. True to his word, our V.P. went forty days with no meat, bread, coffee, or desserts! This brother made and kept a serious fast through the means of a partial fast.

Churches may practice Lent as part of their Easter celebration, and a partial fast is usually employed in connection with the Lenten season.

A partial fast is a very legitimate sacrifice before the Lord and one with which He is pleased.

The Complete Fast

The *complete* or *absolute* fast is the exclusion of all food and drink for a period of time, including water. This fast normally does not last longer than three days due to the fact that the body must have water to survive.

Moses participated in a miraculous complete fast for forty days on the mountain with God (Deut. 9:18). Ezra also did a complete fast when mourning over the unfaithfulness of the exiled Israelites (Ezra 10:6). Both of these are considered miraculous fasts when understanding that they went without food and water for the forty-day period.

In Scripture, there are several examples of the complete fast. Esther, who was from Jewish decent, was married to King Ahasuerus in Susa. Through her uncle, Mordecai, she found out that one of the main servants of her husband, the king, had formed a plot to kill all the Jews in Susa and the surrounding territories. In Esther 4:16, she communicated to Mordecai, "Go, gather together all the Jews who are in Susa, and fast for me. Do not eat or drink for three days, night or day. I and my attendants will fast as you do. When this is done, I will go to the king, even though it is against the law. And if I perish, I perish." In light of the potential tragedy, Esther called for a complete three-day fast.

In the book of Jonah, the king of Nineveh, upon hearing of the coming destruction of his city by God, called for a fast for all who lived there. He issued a decree and stated, "By the decree of the king and his nobles: Do not let people or animals, herds or flocks, taste anything; do not let them eat or drink. But let people and animals be covered with sackcloth. Let everyone call urgently on God. Let them give up their evil ways and their violence" (Jon. 3:7–8).

We also see Saul, who became Paul, on his way to Damascus to persecute believers. Just outside Damascus, Saul experienced a life-changing encounter with Jesus. Jesus appeared to Saul on the road, revealed Himself to him and gave him a message. Temporarily blinded, Saul was led by the hand to Damascus where he waited to hear from the Lord. During the time before Ananias came to Saul, Acts 9:9 tells us that for three days, Saul "was blind, and did not eat or drink." Saul was employing the complete fast as he sought the Lord's will about his future.

When discussing types of fasting, the complete fast is a powerful form of expression. It should be noted that extending the complete fast more than three days may come with certain risks. A person can go for days without food but very few days without water in terms of sustaining health and life. Believers should be mindfully cautious when employing the complete fast.

The Individual Fast

In Scripture, fasting is often done by individuals who seek the Lord in private. It is a time of solitude just between them and the Lord.

David fasted alone on numerous occasions (2 Sam. 12:15–16; 22–23; Ps. 35:13). First Kings 21:27–29 records the occasion where King Ahab fasts by himself. Daniel records his personal fast in Daniel 9:3. Jesus' teaching on fasting in Matthew 6:16–18 indicates fasting individually. Acts 9:9 tells us that Paul fasted alone before God at his conversion.

There will be many occasions when believers simply need to conduct a fast just between themselves and the Lord. This is right and proper as we seek our Father through this means.

National and Group Fasts

The Day of Atonement in Israel was a day set aside in Leviticus 16:29–34 to call the entire nation of Israel to a day of sabbath and rest. They were to dedicate the day to fasting and repentance from their sins. While the Hebrew word for "fasting" is not used in verse 29, Matthew Henry comments, "The phrase 'you shall humble yourselves' or 'you shall afflict your souls' was understood to mean to refrain from all bodily refreshments and delights, in token of inward humiliation and contrition of soul for their sins. On this day, they all fasted from food (except the sick and children) and laid aside their ornaments, and did not anoint themselves."[31] Nehemiah called the sons of Israel together after the walls of Jerusalem were rebuilt and they fasted in repentance before the Lord (Neh. 9:1).

The prophet Joel summoned all of Israel to a fast for repentance when he announced, "Blow a trumpet in Zion, consecrate a fast, proclaim a solemn assembly" (Joel 2:15–17, NASB).

Judah of the divided kingdom was called to a collective fast on a number of occasions.

When King Jehoshaphat discovered that the sons of Moab, along with the sons of Ammon and some of the Meunites were coming to wage war against him, he called all of Judah to a fast for God's protection (2 Chron. 20:1–4).

Ezra, leading his countrymen on a journey, desired protection from the Lord against robbers and enemies. He called a fast among the people for safety and God granted his request (Ezra 8:21–23).

Jeremiah called Judah to fast and repent of their sins in a time of great struggle and stress (Jer. 36:1).

Jonah was called to preach to the pagan city of Nineveh. Much to his surprise, the people began to genuinely repent of their sins. When the king of Nineveh heard of this among the people, he put on sackcloth and sat in ashes (both signs of repentance). As mentioned above, he then proclaimed a complete fast for all people and animals, attempting to avoid the coming punishment from the Lord (Jon. 3:5–9).

Group fasts have taken place in all kinds of circumstances. Nations can be called to fasts by their national leaders. Churches have been called together to fast by their leaders. Christian colleges, universities, and para-church organizations can all call for days of fasting and seeking the Lord. In days marked by sin, declining morals, financial struggles, terrorism, and threats from external as well as internal sources, leaders can call their people together to humble themselves, fast, and pray for God's intervention and blessing. This can and should be done by leaders who understand the power of prayer and fasting.

The Miraculous Fasts

We also find places in Scripture where miraculous fasts take place. These are fasts that occur outside the boundaries of what the human body could tolerate under normal circumstances.

Moses' first miraculous fast is recorded in Deuteronomy 9:9. He described the first time he received the Law on stone tablets from God and his miraculous fast during that experience. He writes, "When I went up to the mountain to receive the tablets of stone, the tablets of the covenant which the Lord had made with you, then I remained on the mountain forty days and nights; I neither ate bread nor drank water" (Deut. 9:9, NASB).

His second miraculous fast was also on Mt. Sinai when he rewrote the tablets himself after destroying them (Ex. 34:27–28). Verse 28 says, "Moses was there with the Lord forty days and forty nights without eating bread or drinking water. And he wrote on the tablets the words of the covenant—the Ten Commandments."

Elijah had done battle with Jezebel and the prophets of Baal. He fled, running for his life and wound up under a juniper tree in the wilderness. He was depressed and asked the Lord to take his life. He fell asleep under the juniper tree and was awakened by an angel who had prepared a bread cake on hot stones and a vessel of water. He ate and drank and fell asleep. This story is repeated again as the angel awakened him and provided another meal. Afterward, we are told, "So he got up and ate and drank. Strengthened by that food, he traveled forty days and forty nights until he reached Horeb, the mountain of God" (1 Kings 19:8). Arthur Wallis observes:

> A journey of such duration through the burning desert, if it was completed as the Scripture implies, without further nourishment, constitutes an absolute fast quite as supernatural as those of Moses. If that be so, it is another striking parallel between these two leading representatives of the old covenant, Moses the giver of the law, and Elijah its restorer (Mal. 4:4–6; Mark 9:12), for both had a supernatural ending to their earthly course, as well

as a supernatural re-appearance with Christ on the holy mount.[32]

It is important to consider the numerous biblical examples of where fasting was utilized and why it was employed. When we grasp both the how and why of fasting, we will be able to understand its impact and implications.

PURPOSES FOR FASTING

When planning a fast, a believer should always have a specific purpose for that fast. Scripture gives us examples for determining purposes for fasting. Let's examine these purposes and bring light to why a Christ follower would enter into a fast.

1. To Fortify Our Prayers

Experiencing prayer and fasting together is seen throughout the Scriptures. To combine fasting with our prayer seems to add strength and impact to our prayer time as we come before the Father. Don Whitney notes, "There's something about fasting that sharpens the edge of our intercessions and gives passion to our supplications. So it has frequently been used by the people of God when there is a special urgency about the concerns they lift before the Father."[33] We might suggest that combining fasting with our prayer brings more weight or increases the intensity of our requests and intercessions. Daniel understood this as he sought the Lord with prayer, supplication, and fasting (Dan. 9:3).

2. To Repent from Sin

When we repent from individual sin in prayer, fasting can accompany our heartfelt repentance. It is appropriate for these two experiences to be presented together before the Lord. David expressed his deep remorse with prayer and fasting in Psalm 69:10. Jonah did the same in Jonah 3:19.

In Dietrich Bonhoeffer's book, *The Cost of Discipleship*, he calls for prayer and fasting in repentance. He writes:

> As soon as a Christian recognizes that he has failed in his service, that his readiness has become feeble, and that he has sinned against another's life and become guilty of another's guilt, that all his joy in God has vanished and that his capacity for prayer has quite gone, it is high time for him to launch an assault upon the flesh, and prepare for better service by fasting and prayer.[34]

Nations can also repent from sin. In the Old Testament, Israel sinned repeatedly in its history. There is a cycle in Israel's history that can be identified in the following manner: God abundantly blesses Israel, Israel falls away from His commands, God sends Israel into bondage, and Israel repents and is restored. As this cycle repeated, Israel's repentance was frequently accompanied by fasting. Leaders of Israel would personally intercede for their people before the Lord, fasting and praying for their restoration. (For specific examples, see Deut. 9:19; 1 Sam. 7:1–6; Ezra 10:6; Neh. 1:4; 9:1–2; Dan. 9:1–6, 9; Joel 2:12–15; Jer. 36:9.) In Jonah 3:5–9, the prophet witnessed the king of Nineveh repenting with fasting over his people and their sin.

3. To Spiritually Prepare for Ministry

Immediately after His public baptism, Jesus was led by the Holy Spirit into the wilderness for a time of fasting and contemplation (Matt. 4:1–11). Many scholars believe that part of Jesus' experience in going to the wilderness was to prepare Himself for His public ministry. His coming work would involve public and private teaching, miracles, and bringing the kingdom of God to man. Seriously seeking His Heavenly Father in the desert and spending time with Him created a spiritual foundation for this coming work.

When believers are called into leadership ministry in the local church, to missionary service, or para-church ministry, an excellent way to begin their service would be to dedicate themselves to a specific time of fasting and prayer. In this time, they seek the Lord for His dynamic presence, blessing, and direction for their coming work. Through fasting, we offer ourselves completely to God without distraction, and we become increasingly aware of His purposes.

4. To Receive Power for Ministry

There is a power that's available to serve Christ far beyond what we can do in the flesh. It is one of the major keys to effective, biblical ministry. Paul, in Ephesians 3:16, prays "that out of his glorious riches he may strengthen you with power through his Spirit in your inner being." We must understand that either we choose to minister in the flesh through our own abilities and our own strength, or we choose to minister through the impacting influence of the Holy Spirit. While effective planning, good strategy, and careful analysis are important, they are secondary to the impact of the Holy Spirit and His presence.

Paul teaches us further in 2 Corinthians 3:5, "Not that we are competent in ourselves to claim anything for ourselves, but our competence comes from God." Again, in 2 Corinthians 4:7, he says, "But we have this treasure in jars of clay to show that this all-surpassing power is from God and not from us."

How do we access this power? We access it through sincere, daily obedience to Christ. We seek Him through soaking prayer and through the ministry of fasting. They are forces that function well beyond hard work and diligence. Ronnie Floyd writes:

God stands at our side, patiently holding yet another connection that promises to link us with one of the greatest sources of power we will ever know. It's a source of power still underused, misunderstood, and even fear-evoking in the minds of some people. Purely and simply, it is the power of God that manifests itself through prayer and fasting.[35]

When we minister through the impact of the Lord's presence, we see results that are significant. When important ministry events happen in the life of our church, severe problems present themselves, or difficult challenges appear, through fasting and prayer we find more than just solutions. We overcome and find victory! All through the presence and power of the Holy Spirit graciously working through us.

My friends, find the power and impact for your service through seeking the Lord in prayer and fasting.

5. To Discover the Lord's Will

There is an "umbrella" will, a universal will that God has for all His people in general.

Scripture gives us clear guidelines as to the Lord's commands and directives: to live a righteous life, to lead others to faith, to serve Him, to obey His commands, to use our spiritual gifts, etc. But there is also God's specific will, revealed to individuals and groups. When discovering God's specific will for our lives, fasting will bring our request for divine guidance directly before the Lord.

We see this demonstrated in numerous places in Scripture. We see this from the sons of Israel praying for guidance in battle (Judg. 20:18–48), to the prayers of a blind Saul in Damascus waiting to discover the Lord's will for his future (Acts 9:9), to the apostles seeking the Lord's guidance in the selection of elders for the early churches (Acts 13:1–4; 14:23).

It is always right to seek the Lord concerning certain, specific areas of our lives. As we pray for wisdom and discernment, we pray and add fasting to the act of seeking the Lord's personal will for each of us. Prior to marriage, whom should we marry? Vocationally, if we receive an offer for a new position, should we take it or remain where we are? Should we sell our house or purchase a house? Whenever we come to a "Y" in the road and need to make a decision, we should go the Lord and ask for His divine guidance. He is our Father. He knows and loves us. He knows what is best for us. We trust Him for His leading through conversations with trusted friends, through confirming signs, and through the guidance of the Holy Spirit and His Word. We pray and fast, asking for His specific direction.

6. To Mourn Those Lost in Death

When loved ones, friends, or acquaintances are lost in death, it is appropriate to fast to express grief. The people of Jabesh-Gilead fasted and mourned at the loss of King Saul (1 Sam. 31:8–13). David also mourned and fasted when he heard of Saul's death and the death of Abner (2 Sam. 1:11–12; 3:31–39). In 2 Samuel 12:15–22, we see David fasting and praying for seven days for the life of the son he was to have with Bathsheba. When the baby passed, David broke his fast. When handling the grief that death brings, we can go to the Lord for comfort and help through a fast.

7. To Seek Protection from Approaching Danger

David, knowing that his strong enemies were near, pleaded with his Father to save him. In Psalm 109:24, he prayed, "My knees give way from fasting; my body is thin and gaunt."

Jonathan, son of Saul, understood that Saul was attempting to kill David. Jonathan grieved over this sin of his father through a fast (1 Sam. 20:30–34).

Ezra was worried about the long trip he was overseeing involving those who had been part of the Babylonian captivity. They had been released to return to Jerusalem. Their trip was around 900 miles! He was worried about enemies and thieves attacking them while they were traveling. Ezra 8:21–23 tells us that a fast was proclaimed for all those making the trip. Through the intercession and fasting of Ezra, the traveling group successfully made the sojourn to Jerusalem.

Just as Ezra interceded for his people, we can also intercede for others in our prayers. Intercessory prayer was offered in the Old Testament by Moses, David, and the Prophets. In the New Testament, Jesus our Lord interceded for His disciples in His High Priestly prayer in John 17. Paul requests in numerous places in his writings prayer from those who loved and supported him. We ask the Lord for help, healing, protection, direction, and blessing on those who need our prayer support. When we intercede for others in our times of prayer and fasting, we are displaying love, mercy, and compassion at the highest levels.

As previously mentioned, Esther also found herself in a very dangerous situation and called a complete fast to save her Jewish countrymen (Esther 4:9–14; 9:1–3).

When we sense that there is grave danger in our lives or futures, going to our Father through a fast is a very wise action. We cling to Him and make our request. The Lord will hear us and move on our behalf.

8. To Accompany Grief in Personal or Corporate Loss

In Nehemiah 1:1–4, we are told that Nehemiah hears of the destruction of Jerusalem. In deep grief over the loss of the city, he enters a time of weeping, mourning, fasting, and prayer. Daniel, grieving the Babylonian captivity that he and his friends were experiencing, calls upon the Lord through fasting and begs God for restoration (Dan. 9:1–6). When Daniel is thrown into the lion's den, King Darius is very disturbed and fasts and stays awake all night, anticipating Daniel's fate (Dan. 6:16–18).

When devastating grief, worry, anxiety, or fear hover over your mind and heart like a dark cloud, or when deep loss becomes part of your journey, turning to the Lord in fasting and prayer can be one of your best first moves. Suffering has a way of focusing our experiences, thinking, and priorities. Turning to the Lord through the fast is what we need to do.

9. To Offer Worship and Praise

The prophetess Anna served "night and day" in the temple, offering up "fasting and praying" (Luke 2:36–38). Her ministry of prayer and fasting was acceptable to God as her service and work. Fasting in our private times of worship and praise impacts our experience with the Father. It can be such a rich time in His presence. When we are together corporately, we offer up a wonderful and sweet sacrifice of adoration and worship through our singing and praying. We listen to the Word of God proclaimed, offer our material resources, and meet Jesus around His table in celebrating the Lord's Supper. These worship expressions are all enhanced through the offering up of the fast. Fasting seems to *intensify* the worship experience. It helps to draw us closer to our Father as we present ourselves to Him in a heartfelt time of personal and corporate worship.

10. To Avert God's Wrath

Wrath can be described as an emotional response to perceived wrong and injustice. It is often expressed with anger, indignation, or irritation. God's wrath is a very real part of who He is. We need to always remember that along with the overflowing grace of God, there are dark lines in His face as well. John Stott describes God's wrath as "His steady, unrelenting, unremitting, uncompromising antagonism to evil in all its forms and manifestations."[36] His wrath is revealed dramatically in the Old Testament when Israel repeatedly sinned through their disobedience (Exod. 32:11; Deut. 11:17; Ps. 89:46). The New Testament also describes God's wrath, which is provoked through blatant sin and rebellion (Rom. 1:18; 2:5). His wrath is taken away through sincere repentance.

There may be times when a nation, state, city, church, family, or individual can evoke the wrath of God due to sin. As we repent through fasting and prayer, God meets us in His grace and forgives us.

11. To Set Aside People for Ministry Leadership

The early church prayed and fasted when setting aside specific people for leadership work. In Acts 14:23, elders for the church were being appointed. We should note that prayer and fasting were part of this process. In Acts 13:2–3, Paul and Barnabas were being set aside for missionary service. Again, the church fasted and prayed over this event. These two elements were absolutely essential to leadership selection.

The reason is evident. As the leaders of any church or para-church organization go, so goes that church or organization. The leadership team determines whether that church or organization has a healthy culture and whether it is completing its assigned mission. The leaders set the pace and example of faith and practice. When the leadership team of a church is competent, the church moves forward. A great deal of the organization's effectiveness is determined by who is leading the church. This is why seeking the Lord through prayer and fasting before selecting significant leaders was so important in the early church. Soaking prayer and sincere fasting should always be a part of any leadership selection in the body of Christ.

As you can see, there are numerous excellent reasons to fast. Are you ready to begin incorporating fasting into your relationship with God? Next, we will explore how to start.

HOW TO PLAN A FAST

There are several important ideas to consider when planning a fast. Considering each one will contribute to a positive and impactful time of fasting.

Step 1 – *Be Aware of the Spirit's Promptings*

When you plan a fast, there may be a specific need to be addressed or you may feel the promptings of the Holy Spirit. The Lord may be calling you to stand in the gap for someone or to minister to a critical need. The need may also be your own. Sense the Holy Spirit's leading when it is time to plan a fast.

Ronnie Floyd gives good direction about what to do at the beginning of a fast. He shares, "One of the most important things to do prior to a fast is to ask God what He wants to accomplish during this intense time with Him."[37] Seeking the Lord about what He wants to have happen gives great direction to a successful fasting experience.

Step 2 – *Make a Specific Commitment to Complete the Fast*

You have decided to conduct a fast. "Drive a stake," and make the decision that you will see your fast through to completion. You will usually be tempted to break your fast early but stay true to your decision to finalize your fast. Decide before you begin to make it a positive and complete commitment to the Lord.

Step 3 – *Communicate to Those Who Need to Know*

Communicate to your spouse or others who would need to know your fasting plan in terms of meal preparation, schedule, etc. Showing consideration to others in your life indicates good planning and thoughtfulness.

Step 4 – *Select a Specific Purpose*

For what specific purpose are you planning the fast? To offer worship, to intercede for someone, for repentance, to seek the Lord's will and direction? Be sure to identify the reason or reasons for which you will be fasting. Then during your fasting hours, focus on that singular purpose or multiple purposes.

Step 5 – *Determine the Length of Your Fast*

A good fast should always have a time frame. You can fast through one meal, two meals, a twenty-four hour fast, or longer. Fasting through breakfast would mean missing the first meal of the day and then having lunch at noon. Fasting through lunch would mean that you enjoy breakfast, fast through lunch and then break your fast with dinner. A twenty-four hour fast would last from one day to the next day.

For beginners, start slowly by beginning with one meal. You could then increase to two meals or to a twenty-four hour fast. In time, move to a thirty-six hour fast and, when you are ready, to a forty-eight hour fast. Then possibly a three-day fast and on from there. There are examples in Scripture of people fasting one night, a full day, three days, seven days, fourteen days, twenty-one days, and forty days. Determining the length of your fast provides organization and clarity to the experience.

Also know this, there is never a "convenient time" to conduct a fast. There are places to be, schedules to keep, and appointments to fulfill. We are convinced that Satan will wage war against any and every attempt you make to meet the Lord in the fast. This is why making a decision, setting a date, and making it happen are so important.

Step 6 – *Decide on the Type of Fast*

Would you like to do a normal fast with no food or drink with a caloric value? Or would a partial fast be best? Or do you want to do a complete fast? Decide on the type of fast that best fits your present situation, circumstances, and occasion.

Step 7 – *Start Your Fast with Repentance and Confession*

Why not begin your fast with a serious time of seeking the Lord through repentance from sin? It could be a time of spiritual cleansing and purification. In Richard Foster's excellent work *Prayer: Finding the Heart's True Home,* he discusses the Prayer of Examine. In the Prayer of Examine, one does a thorough "spiritual housecleaning." Foster says:

> In the examine of conscience we are inviting the Lord to search our hearts to the depths. Far from being dreadful, this is a scrutiny of love. We boldly speak the words of the Psalmist, "Search me, O God, and know my heart; test me and know my thoughts. See if there is any wicked way in me, and lead me in the way everlasting" (Ps. 139:23–24). Without apology and without defense we ask to see what is truly in us. It is for our own sake that we ask these things. It is for our good, for our healing, for our happiness.[38]

Let us begin our fast through the Lord's cleansing from sin and present ourselves pure through the blood of Jesus.

Step 8 – *Fill Your Heart with Scripture*

During your fast, if possible, take in meaningful sections of the Word. Read chapters or entire books, if time allows. Filling your heart with the Word of God will nurture your soul and spirit. Take advantage of this important discipline as your circumstances allow. It is one of the most important parts of deepening your fasting experience.

Step 9 – *Pray Fervently and Often*

Prayer should be a major part of your fasting experience. This is one of the necessary elements of a fast. During a fast, we seek our Father, we spend time with Him, we engage Him, we communicate clearly and specifically with Him, we soak Him up, and we enjoy His presence. Be sure to plan as much time with the Father as possible during this sacred time.

Step 10 – *Times of Solitude and Silence*

It is in silence and solitude that we close out the world and the din that comes with it and focus on our Father. We connect specifically with Him heart-to-heart as much as time allows. If you are fasting during a workday, this may not be possible. But when opportunities present themselves for silence and solitude, do use these important disciplines for a very meaningful time of fellowship with our Father.

Step 11 – *Know the Lord Is Pleased*

Scripture tells us that we can please the Lord as His children. One of the times we know the Lord is pleased with us is when we successfully complete a fast. We have voluntarily given up or set aside something important to us to focus on Him. Like a father proud of His children, He recognizes our commitment and expression of love through our fast.

FASTING AND HEALTH

There are many excuses people give for not fasting, some related to health concerns. People can be worried that fasting is dangerous because they think it can throw the body out of whack or cause their blood sugar to bottom out. People express concerns that they don't want to go into starvation mode and lose muscle. There are probably more excuses but those are a few of the top reasons.

I (Mike) have been a physician's assistant for over twenty-five years and the human body fascinates me. It fascinates me because it screams creation in so many ways—everything from the way blood clots to the way a body heals itself when injured. In previous sections, we have talked about biblical occasions and reasons for fasting and now we would like to briefly explore some of the science behind fasting. God has designed our bodies in a way in which fasting not only draws us closer to Him but is also good for us physically. This spiritual practice which people have used for thousands of years is increasingly validated by scientific study.

Medically speaking, the results of fasting show that it has favorable results on the body and mind. There is a large misconception in the general population that fasting is dangerous and not good for people physically. Actually, the medical community has discovered that fasting is quite safe for people without medical conditions which would not allow fasting. Far from fasting being a practice which harms our bodies, the evidence shows that fasting benefits the body in many ways. In his book *The Obesity Code*, Dr. Jason Fung, a modern expert on human metabolism and hormonal interplay, writes, "Fasting is one of the oldest remedies in human history and has been part of virtually every culture and religion on earth."[39] Further, Dr. Fung notes that several positive things happen in the body during fasting. Research shows that fasting reduces insulin levels, improves insulin sensitivity, lowers the body of excess salt, increases growth hormones, increases the body's utilization of fats for fuel, and increases adrenaline. He states that this answers the two unspoken questions. "Is it unhealthy?" The answer is no. Scientific studies conclude that fasting carries significant health benefits. Metabolism increases, energy increases, and blood sugars decrease. The only remaining question is this: "Can you do it?" . . . . Absolutely 100% yes."[40]

As Dr. Fung points out, while fasting, the body adapts to alternative fuel sources such as breaking down fatty acids for the necessary energy the body needs. The only time it appears unhealthy is if one's body fat percentage is dangerously low to begin with.

According to Dr. Don Colbert's book *Toxic Relief: Restore Health and Energy through Fasting and Detoxifi-*

cation Colbert shows how fasting is key to detoxing. He says: "Fasting is a dynamic key to cleansing your body from a lifetime collection of toxins, reversing inflammation, over-nourishment and the diseases they bring, and ensuring a wonderful future of renewed energy, vitality, longevity, and blessed health."[41] As you consider adding fasting to your lifestyle, it is important to remember that water is crucial. Water is vital to human life and should not be withheld for long periods of time (greater than twenty-four hours). Water is necessary to maintain basic cellular mechanisms and proper organ functions. Personally, during fasts, I (Mike) like to allow water and fluids like coffee or tea without additives such as sugar or creamer. This helps to avoid the headaches that can come from caffeine withdrawal. During hot weather, I also like to drink water containing electrolytes. When I drink water during a fast, I often use the moment as a reminder that Jesus promised to give us "living water" (John 7:38).

Fasting that is well-planned and done with care can be of great value to us physically. When starting the fasting discipline, possibly for the first time, be sure to consider the following:

- Check with your doctor, especially if you are on daily medications for your health.
- If you are diabetic or hypoglycemic, do follow the doctor's orders about how to navigate this issue.

If fasting from food is a problem, you may choose other ways to participate in the fast.

- If you are pregnant, plan on finding a way to fast that does not involve eliminating food.

- If you have struggled with any eating disorder in the past or at present, do talk to someone who can advise you about carefully navigating this situation.

- If you are involved in high energy or high physically demanding work, especially during summer heat, be careful about the fasting regimen and how to conduct it.

- There are definitely physical factors involved during a fast. Be aware of these: fatigue, possible headache, sleepiness, mild dizziness. These are temporary and will subside when your fast is over.

- When breaking a fast of 24–48 hours, begin slowly by taking fruit or vegetable juices, a leafy green salad, or a baked potato. When breaking longer fasts, be very careful to start eating again slowly. Begin with bland foods such as salads with no dressing, baked or sweet potatoes, and soups. Do not take fatty or greasy foods for several days to allow your system to adjust to food again. The key is to go slowly and take your time re-entering.

QUESTIONS AND ANSWERS

1. *How do I know when it is time to conduct a fast?* If it is a group fast, the occasion will determine the fast. If it is personal, be open to the leading of the Holy Spirit. Needs and situations may also determine when a fast is necessary. For example, if you are considering taking a new position in a city 300 miles away, the presentation of this opportunity could determine your need for a fast.

2. *What if I get extremely hungry in the middle of my fast? What should I do?* Let your hunger pangs bring you back to the purpose of your fast. Understand that hunger is part of a fast. I (David) have found that drinking a large glass of water helps assuage hunger temporarily. It also is important in terms of hydration while you are fasting.

3. *Once I set a time for my fast, is it okay to break the fast early?* You really shouldn't. Setting a time for a fast is somewhat like taking a vow before our Father. To plan a proper fasting experience, we need to set parameters to ensure the success of the fast. So don't break your fast early even though you may be tempted to do so.

4. *How do I handle the anonymity (not letting others know) of fasting, for example, when I am married or have a boss who enjoys having a weekly lunch together?* When Jesus taught about fasting in Matthew 6, He

was mainly referring to the heart of the religious leaders of the day who had very impure motives for why they were fasting. Are you telling others about the fast so that they will think highly of you? The motive in your heart for why you are sharing about your fast is the key to Jesus' teaching. There may be people whom you need to talk to as you plan a fast.

5. *Can you take fruit or vegetable juices when fasting?* When you are participating in a shorter fast (one to two days,) you may want to do without. Fasts lasting longer that forty-eight hours may allow for juices, hot or cold decaffeinated teas, bouillon, thin soups, etc. Be careful to avoid fruit or vegetable juices with a high acid content such as orange or tomato juice which may be hard on the stomach. Juiced fresh fruits and vegetables such as apples, grapes, lemons, beets, carrots, celery, or cabbage are all good. Do not chew gum or mints as they will start the stomach's digestive processes.

6. *Can I continue my physical training and workouts while fasting?* You can, on a limited basis. You may want to cut your workouts back somewhat or altogether for a time. Listen to your body and be aware of how you need to handle physical exercise. Moderation is key here.

God is constantly calling us to a new level of growth and forward movement. Like any other loving parent, His desire for each child is that we grow to a positive level of maturity. Fasting is one of the elements that enables us to grow in our spiritual journeys. God wants to nurture us and wants to see us thrive. He desires that we have everything that He has planned for us as His children. He wants us to have the fasting experience to receive all the joy and stimulation that this discipline provides. Don Whitney reminds us:

> Like all the Spiritual Disciplines, fasting hoists the sails of the soul in hopes of experiencing the gracious wind of God's Spirit. But fasting also adds a unique dimension to your spiritual life and helps you grow in Christlikeness in ways that are unavailable through any other means. If this were not so, there would have been no need for Jesus to model and teach fasting.[42]

Friends, pursue and plan times of fasting in your personal regimen. It is a wonderful, stretching, and nurturing way to come close to our Father and grow in His grace. Make it part of your journey and your God-saturated adventure of growing in Christ!

DISCUSSION QUESTIONS

1. In your own words, share a definition for the concept of *fasting*.

2. Have you participated in a personal fast? Can you share details about this experience?

3. How would you decide on which type of fast (normal, partial or complete) to use when starting a fast?

4. Have you ever started a fast and wound up breaking that fast early? Can you share what happened to cause you to break that fast early?

5. What is the hardest aspect to face and conquer when starting a fast?

6. If you were to do a partial fast (the giving up of only certain food(s)), what would you give up and why?

7. If you have previously fasted, what were the specific benefits you experienced from your fast(s)?

8. From previous fasts, share the most difficult stress you faced in keeping your fast to the end of the designated time.

9. Out of the reasons to fast listed in this section (see pages 69–79), which reasons would be the most likely to draw you into a personal fast?

10. What is the connection between fasting and discovering the Lord's will for your personal life?

11. In addition to food and drink, what other things could you temporarily remove to express a credible

fast to the Lord? (television, sports, electronics, people, etc.) Which would be the hardest?

12. What have you specifically learned about yourself and your life in Christ from your fasting experiences?

FINAL REFLECTIONS

I t is natural that we would write a book combining prayer and fasting. Faithful believers throughout biblical history paired the two together. Consider the following Scriptures:

- So we *fasted* and *petitioned* our God about this, and he answered our prayer (Ezra 8:23).
- When I heard these things, I sat down and wept. For some days I mourned and *fasted* and *prayed* before the God of heaven (Neh. 1:4).
- So I turned to the Lord God and pleaded with him in *prayer* and petition, in *fasting*, and in sackcloth and ashes (Dan. 9:3).
- She never left the temple but worshiped night and day, *fasting* and *praying* (Luke 2:37).
- So after they had *fasted* and *prayed*, they placed their hands on them and sent them off (Acts 13:3).
- Paul and Barnabas appointed elders for them in each church and, with *prayer* and *fasting*, committed them to the Lord, in whom they had put their trust (Acts 14:23).

God-focused, self-denying prayer and fasting is countercultural, but it is a trail blazed by faithful believers who have gone before us. They prayed, fasted, and saw God do great things in response. *Will you join them?*

Let us say that we are preparing to board a sailing vessel of yesteryear for an important trip. The ship has no mechanical power, depending just on the wind. We board the ship. The cargo plus other passengers, crew, and supplies needed for the trip are brought aboard. All is prepared, the sails are all hoisted, and we are ready to depart. But there is one necessary ingredient we are awaiting. It is the wind. It is the power of the wind which will provide the driving force behind our successful trip. As the wind picks up, the ship begins to move forward. The sails billow with the driving winds, taking the ship to our expected port.

In this simple analogy, the ship is the church. What is the wind? The wind is the presence of the Holy Spirit coming to fill the sails of the church, sending it to complete its intended mission. We long for the day when our Father will send the winds of the Spirit to revive and empower the church! We long to experience a major prayer movement in action, forging forward through the power of the Holy Spirit. As we humble ourselves with steadfast prayer and regular fasting, we can and should expect impacting things to happen. This path of prayer and fasting needs to become more than something we read about; we need to devote ourselves to this path as we seek the Lord and His goodness, blessing, and power.

Through this book, we want to encourage you to move to the next level in your spiritual journey when it comes to the disciplines of prayer and fasting. In terms of prayer, we would encourage you to remember some key insights from this book: God finds delight in our prayers. Although prayer is surrounded by spiritual warfare, we must persevere to make prayer a serious priority for our lives and ministries. We must incorporate prayer into our schedules (regular time and place). We must truly believe that prayer makes a difference. And, instead of putting prayer off until things settle down, we must just begin.

In terms of fasting, recall that starting slowly and moving forward is the best way to learn this discipline. Use the fast as an opportunity to repent and pray. When you think through the various reasons to fast, you will recognize fasting as a needed discipline in our time. There is much to mourn and repent of. We can sense confusion about God's will and a sense of danger about what is on the horizon. As always, "The harvest is plentiful but the workers are few" (Matt. 9:37), and we need to fast and pray for God to send ministry workers out into His harvest field. The discipline of fasting is a powerful force as we present ourselves, our worship, and our requests to the Lord.

Prayer and fasting are two powerful aspects which bring us into God's presence, allow us to find His favor, and open doors to be used by Him in a powerful way. Move forward with complete confidence that the Lord is with you, and may we see Spirit-fueled revival in our times.

BIBLIOGRAPHY

1. Ronnie Floyd, *The Power of Prayer and Fasting: The Power of Prayer and Fasting* (Nashville: Broadman and Holman, 1997), 20–21.

2. Greg Pruitt, *Extreme Prayer: The Impossible Prayers God Promises to Answer* (Carol Stream: Tyndale House, 2014), 5, 7.

3. Richard Foster, *Celebration of Discipline: The Path to Spiritual Growth* (New York: Harper and Row, 1988), 33.

4. E.M. Bounds, *E. M. Bounds on Prayer* (Grand Rapids: Baker Books, 1990), 256–257.

5. Tim Keller, *Prayer: Experiencing Awe and Intimacy with God* (New York: Penguin Books, 2014), 27.

6. E.M. Bounds, *E. M. Bounds on Prayer* (Grand Rapids: Baker Books, 1990), 244.

7. David Butts, Forgotten Power: *A Simple Theology for a Praying Church* (Terre Haute: PrayerShop Publishing, 2015), 50.

8. Samuel Chadwick, as quoted in David Butts, *Forgotten Power* (Terre Haute: PrayerShop Publishing, 2015), 50–51.

9. Interview with Dr. Bare at Camp Como, Como, CO, June, 1984.

10. Martha Thatcher, *The Freedom of Obedience* (Colorado Springs: NavPress, 1987), 13.

11. C.S. Lewis, *The Four Loves* (New York, Harcourt and Brace, 1960), 13.

12. Jean Fleming, as quoted in John Piper, *Desiring God: Meditations of a Christian Hedonist* (Sisters, OR: Multnomah, 1996), 156.

13. John Piper, *Desiring God* (Sisters, OR: Multnomah Publishers, 1996), 156.

14. C.S. Lewis, *The Business of Heaven: Daily Readings* (New York: Harcourt and Brace, 1984)

15. F.F. Bruce, *The New International Commentary on the New Testament* (Grand Rapids: Eerdmans Publishers, 1984), 330.

16. E.M. Bounds, *E.M. Bounds on Prayer* (Grand Rapids: Baker Books, 1990), 447.

17. Bill Hybels, *Too Busy Not to Pray: Slowing Down to Be with God* (Downers Grove: IVP, 1998), 15–16.

18. Emilie Griffin, *Clinging: The Experience of Prayer* (New York: Harper and Row, 1984), 1.

19. Richard Foster, *Celebration of Discipline: The Path to Spiritual Growth* (New York: Harper and Row, 1978), 39–40.

20. See *God's Chosen Fast* by Arthur Wallis (Fort Washington: Christian Literature Crusade, 2015), *The Power of Prayer and Fasting* by Ronnie Floyd (New York: Broadman and Holman, 1997), *The Miracle of Fasting: Proven throughout History for Physical, Mental, and Spiritual Rejuvenation* by Patricia Bragg and Paul C. Bragg (Bragg Health Sciences, 2004), and *The Breakthrough Guide to Fasting* by Elmer Towne (Bloomington: Bethany House Publishers, 2013), plus many other excellent works on the topic.

21. "Spiritual Disciplines: A Practical Strategy," *Renovare*. https://renovare.org/about/ideas/spiritual-disciplines (accessed June 25, 2020).

22. Ronnie Floyd, *The Power of Prayer and Fasting: The Power of Prayer and Fasting* (Nashville: Broadman and Holman, 1997), 3.

23. Donald Whitney, *Spiritual Disciplines for the Christian Life* (Colorado Springs, CO: NavPress, 1991), 152.

24. "Chapter II Biblical Perspective of Fasting and Its Development through the Inter-Testamental and Post Biblical Period," *AP Messiah Party Nepal*, July 12, 2012. http://apmessiahparty.blogspot.com/2012/07/chapter-ii-biblical-perspecive-of.html (accessed June 25, 2020).

25. "Fasting," *Encyclopedia Britannica*, https://www.britannica.com/topic/fasting (accessed June 25, 2020).

26. Martin Lloyd Jones, *Studies in the Sermon on the Mount* (Grand Rapids: Eerdmans, 1960), vol. 1, 38.

27. D.A. Carson, *The Expositor's Bible Commentary*, vol. 8 (Grand Rapids: Zondervan, 1984), 175.

28. Ronnie Floyd, *The Power of Prayer and Fasting: The Power of Prayer and Fasting* (Nashville: Broadman and Holman, 1997), 139.

29. Richard Foster, *Celebration of Discipline: The Path to Spiritual Growth* (New York: Harper and Row, 1988), 53–54. (For additional information on the particular text of Matt. 9:14–17, see Foster, 52–54.)

30. Arthur Wallis, *God's Chosen Fast* (Fort Washington: Christian Literature Crusade, 1971), 13–14.

31. Mathew Henry, *Matthew Henry's Commentary on the Whole Bible*, Vol. 1 (McLean: MacDonald Publishing Co, 1706), 508. (While the Hebrew word for fasting is not formally found in verse 29, the Standard Hebrew Lexicon, Oxford, 1975, authors Brown, Driver and Briggs confirm the use of the Hebrew word "fasting" as an acceptable translation for "humble" or "afflict.")

32. Arthur Wallis, *God's Chosen Fast* (Fort Washington: Christian Literature Crusade, 1971), 16.

33. Donald Whitney, *Spiritual Disciplines for the Christian Life* (Colorado Springs: NavPress, 1991), 157.

34. Dietrich Bonhoeffer, *The Cost of Discipleship*, translated by Chrs. Kaiser Verlag (London: SCM Press, 2015), 116.

35. Ronnie Floyd, *The Power of Prayer and Fasting: The Power of Prayer and Fasting* (Nashville: Broadman and Holman, 1997), 2.

36. John Stott, *The Cross of Christ* (Downers Grove: InterVarsity, 2006), 171.

37. Ronnie Floyd, *The Power of Prayer and Fasting: The Power of Prayer and Fasting* (Nashville: Broadman and Holman, 1997), xxii.

38. Richard Foster, *Prayer: Finding the Heart's True Home* (New York: HarperCollins, 1992), 29.

39. Jason Fung, *The Obesity Code: Unlocking the Secrets of Weight Loss* (Vancouver: Greystone Books, 2016), 236.

40. Ibid, 249.

41. Don Colbert, *Toxic Relief: Restore Health and Energy through Fasting and Detoxification*, revised and expanded (Lake Mary: Siloam, 2012), 44.

42. Donald Whitney, *Spiritual Disciplines for the Christian Life* (Colorado Springs: NavPress, 1991), 171.

ABOUT THE AUTHORS

DR. DAVID ROADCUP is Professor of Discipleship and Global Outreach Representative for TCM International in Indianapolis, IN. He has been in ministry for over fifty-four years. Besides youth ministries, senior ministries, preaching ministries, and college and seminary teaching through the years, Dr. Roadcup has authored numerous articles, four books, and has tri-authored a series of nine books on the eldership of the church. He is a graduate of Lincoln Christian University, Lincoln, IL (B.A. in Christian Ministries), Cincinnati Christian University, Cincinnati, Ohio (M.A. in Pastoral Counseling), and Trinity Evangelical Divinity School, Deerfield, IL (D.Min. in Christian Ministries). He has spoken in thirty-seven states and eighteen foreign countries. As one of the founding members of the men's ministry Promise Keepers, he served on its Board of Directors for eleven years. In 2001, he was on the summer P.K. Men's Conference Speaking Team. He is one of the three founding members of the elder training ministry e2 Elders located in Indianapolis, IN. Together, the e2 team has authored nine books and additional training materials for elder training in the church. This ministry has trained over 8,000 elders nationwide. He is presently on the Board of Directors of Christ in Youth in Joplin, Missouri (C.I.Y.) and the Board of Directors of Christian Arabic Services (C.A.S.). He has been married to Karen for fifty-three years. Dave and Karen have two married daughters and four grandchildren. Dave works in the areas of relational discipling, spiritual formation, church growth and health, evangelism, and leadership in the church. His great passion lies in discipling believers and helping Christians grow to deeper levels in their personal walks with Jesus Christ.

MICHAEL EAGLE has worked for twenty-seven years as a physician assistant in orthopedic surgery at hospitals such as Mayo Clinic and Vanderbilt University Medical School. He is an ex-marathon runner (having run eighteen marathons) and has completed two Ironman Events. He has an interest in nutrition and exercise and how it relates to the human body (thus, the medical perspective of fasting in this book). Jesus fully took a hold of Mike in his late 30s and did an overhaul on his heart, mind, and soul. In Mike's journey to know Jesus more fully, he embarked on a journey that took him through a three-year ordination course through Harpeth Christian Church. He was ordained as an elder and was inspired to further his education in theological studies through TCM International where he completed a discipleship program and is finishing up his master's degree. It is there where he first met David Roadcup, who was teaching on discipleship. When tasked with writing a research paper on a spiritual discipline, he found that fasting stood out as something he wanted to know more about. As he spent more time in research, he was convicted that God was illuminating an art so beautiful and profound that he couldn't understand why the American church did not know more about it. His curiosity about fasting became a passion, and together with David, he is humbled and honored to write this book to help fuel a renewal of prayer and fasting—a renewal which will help fuel revival in our world. Mike has been married to Michelle for twenty-six years, and they have two children, Courtney and Mason.

Made in the USA
Columbia, SC
13 September 2022